PAPER

Andrew Langley

Consultants: Scott Limited

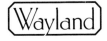

Titles in this series

Bricks	Plastics
Glass	Steel
Oil	Water
Paper	Wood

Cover: (Main picture) Paper is wound on to big reels when it comes off the papermaking machine. (Top right) Pulp logs for paper.

Editor: Sarah Doughty

First published in 1991 by
Wayland (Publishers) Ltd
61 Western Road, Hove
East Sussex, BN3 1JD, England

British Library Cataloguing in Publication Data
Langley, Andrew
   Paper. — (Links)
   I. Title II. Series
   676

ISBN 0 7502 0157 6

Typeset by Dorchester Typesetting Group Ltd
Printed in Italy by G. Canale & C.S.p.A.

Contents

Paper is everywhere   4

What is paper made of?   6

Paper in history   8

Growing trees   10

The pulp mill   12

Preparing the pulp   14

Rolling and drying   16

Using paper   18

Boards and boxes   20

New paper from old   22

The world's forests   24

Paper and pollution   26

Projects with paper   28

Glossary   30

Books to read   31

Index   32

All the words that appear in **bold** are explained in the glossary on page 30.

Paper is everywhere

There is paper everywhere. Look around and see how much we use. We read newspapers and books made of paper. We write and draw on paper. Food comes wrapped in paper or packed in cardboard boxes. We use paper to make tissues, paper towels, labels, stamps, sticky tape and paper money. Word processors and computers use paper to print out information.

Huge reels of paper in store at a paper mill. The paper may be used to make stationery, books and magazines.

4

A few of the many products that are made from paper.

We can also find paper in some surprising places. Car engines have paper filters which keep the oil and air clean. Other special types of paper are used in fireworks, television sets and even in the hulls of boats.

Why is paper so useful? One reason is that it is cheap to make. It can also be made very soft or very strong. Paper can be coloured, or coated to make it waterproof. Paper is easy to use because it is light, and simple to bend and cut. When paper has been used, it can be pulped again and made into fresh paper.

What is paper made of?

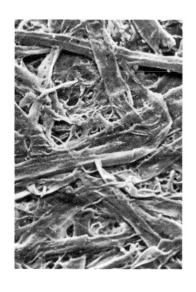

Look closely at a piece of newspaper, and you will see hundreds of tiny hairs. These are **fibres** of **cellulose**. They are matted together to make a thin, flat sheet. If the fibres are wetted, they become soft, and the paper falls apart. But as they dry they tangle together, and become stiff and strong.

This magnified picture of uncoated paper shows how the fibres of cellulose mat together.

Nearly all the world's paper is made from wood. Wood is cheap and easy to grow. It is chopped up and 'cooked' to make millions of tiny fibres, each less than 1mm long. This is called wood **pulp**.

Logs are cut into chips before they are pulped to make paper.

Other materials are also used in papermaking. Cotton and linen rags have fine fibres, which can be made into high quality paper. Art paper and legal documents are often made of rags.

Bank notes are printed on high-quality paper made from cotton and linen rags.

Hemp and manila are thick grassy plants from Asia. They have coarse fibres, and are used to make strong wrapping paper and envelopes. Coarse paper is also made from straw.

Paper in history

Above *Paper-making was introduced into China in AD 105 by T'sai Lun.*

Paper gets its name from **papyrus**. This is a reed which grows in the River Nile. The Ancient Egyptians made writing materials by cutting the papyrus into thin strips and weaving it into sheets.

Nearly 1,900 years ago, a Chinaman named T'sai Lun made the first proper paper. He mixed up bark, old fishing nets, rags and rope with water, and spread the pulp out to dry.

Right *A method of making papyrus based on the technique of the Ancient Egyptians.*

8

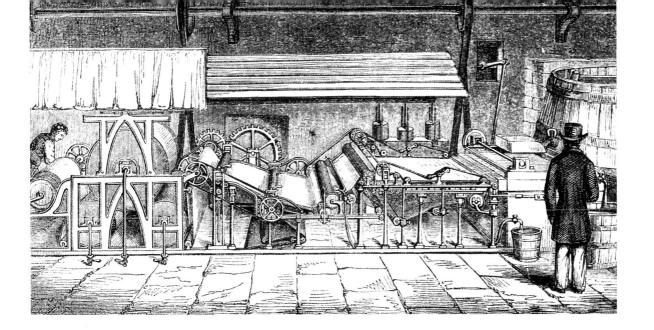

The art of papermaking spread across the world and remained unchanged for centuries. When printing began in Europe in 1455, there was suddenly a huge demand for paper. But it had to be made by hand using old rags, so the process was messy and slow.

In 1798 a Frenchman invented the first papermaking machine. It produced paper in long sheets, much more quickly than by hand. Soon, there were not enough rags to pulp, and papermakers began to use wood pulp instead. Since then, paper has become one of the most important products in the world.

This early papermaking machine was built several years after the first French machine of 1798, and was more successful.

Growing trees

Softwood plantations of coniferous forest provide wood for paper.

Without forests, and their millions of trees, we would have very little paper. So forests have to be looked after and harvested carefully. Most forests are specially planted to provide pulp for papermaking.

Foresters look after the growing trees. They must make sure that there is always a supply of wood for cutting. Young trees are grown in nurseries. They are then planted in fields where they need to be protected from pests and diseases.

There are two main kinds of trees. **Softwoods** have needle-like leaves and bear cones. **Hardwoods** have broad leaves, which they shed in autumn. Paper is usually made from softwood trees, but sometimes a mixture of hardwoods and softwoods is used.

A team of loggers cuts down the trees with chain-saws. They trim off the branches and twigs and collect them up. The logs are carried out of the forest by truck, or by being floated down a nearby river.

Above Logs being floated down the river, near Washington, USA.

Left A logger felling a tree with a chain-saw.

The pulp mill

Once the logs are cut, they are taken to the pulp mill. Pulp mills are usually built near forest areas. First, the logs are put into a giant drum. The drum spins round, and steel blades inside tear the bark from the logs.

The wood then goes into the **chipper**. This is a huge mincing machine which grinds up the wood into small chips. The chips travel to another big vat, where they are mixed with water and chemicals. The mixture is heated

A diagram showing how wood is made into pulp at the pulp mill.

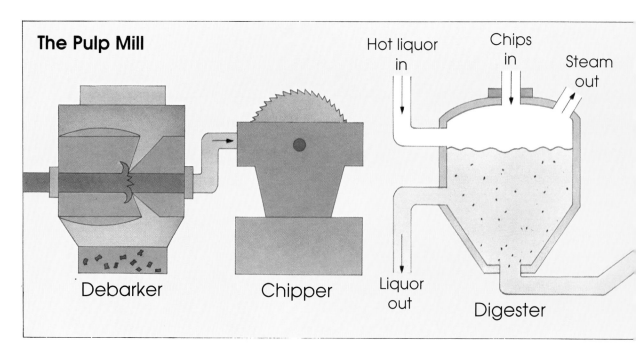

The Pulp Mill

Hot liquor in

Chips in

Steam out

Debarker

Chipper

Liquor out

Digester

and `cooked´ until it turns into a mushy pulp.

Next, the pulp is cleaned. It is whirled round in a big drum. The heavy lumps and **knots** drop to the bottom, and the pure pulp comes out at the top. Sometimes the pulp is **bleached**. This makes the pulp whiter and purifies it. The bleach is washed out with water.

The pulp is now ready to be made into paper. But the paper mill may be far away. So the pulp is dried into sheets and packed in bales before being transported to the paper mill.

Above *Pulp mills such as this one in Vancouver, Canada are usually built near forest areas.*

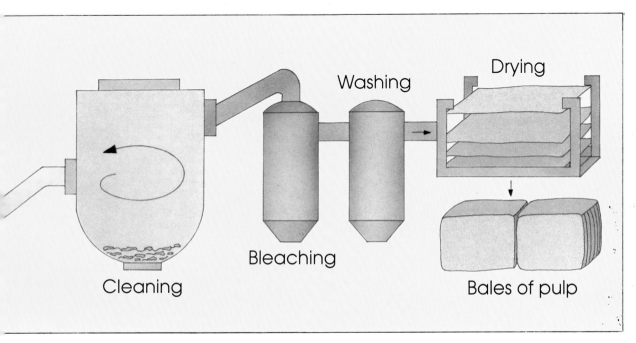

Cleaning

Bleaching

Washing

Drying

Bales of pulp

Preparing the pulp

At the paper mill, the dried bales of wood pulp are turned back into a liquid. The bales are broken up and mashed with water. Sometimes waste paper is also added to the mixture.

The fibres in the mashed pulp are still too stiff. They must be fluffed out, so that they will bind together well and make strong paper. The pulp is put into a

The wood pulp arrives at the paper mill packed into bales.

The sheets of wood pulp are broken up and mixed with water to make a liquid.

refiner, which has a cone-shaped beater covered with bars. It turns very fast, and the bars beat the pulp into a smooth, watery liquid.

Other materials are now added to the mixture. These include **size**, clay and colouring. Size is a kind of glue which stops the paper from soaking up too much ink when it is used. Clay fills up the tiny gaps between the fibres. This makes the paper whiter and less transparent. The paper can also be coloured with dye.

The paper is coloured by adding inks or dyes.

Rolling and drying

At one end of the papermaking machine the fibres of pulp tangle together and the water drains away.

Paper is rolled and dried on a papermaking machine. At one end of the machine is the **flow head**. This is a box which spreads a thin layer of pulp on to a moving mesh. The **mesh** shakes from side to side, to help the fibres tangle together as the water drains away.

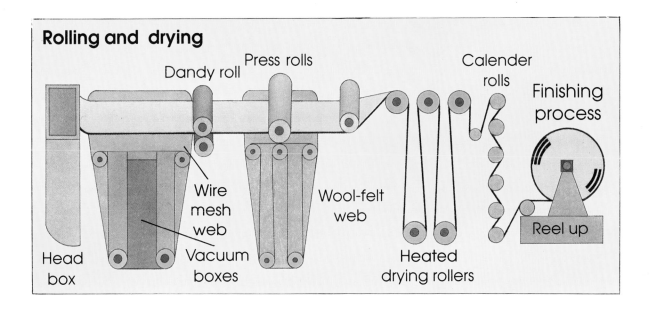

Rolling and drying

Head box · Dandy roll · Press rolls · Wire mesh web · Vacuum boxes · Wool-felt web · Heated drying rollers · Calender rolls · Finishing process · Reel up

Some water from the pulp drains out through the mesh. More is sucked out by **vacuum boxes** underneath. As the water drains, the pulp forms into a sheet. Soon it is strong enough to be lifted off the mesh.

The sheet is still very soggy. For most papers it is squeezed by a series of rollers. The first rollers are solid and heavy and squeeze the paper dry. The next set of rollers are hollow, and heated inside by steam to dry the paper. Cold rollers, called **calenders**, give the paper a final polish. The paper comes off the machine and is wound on to a giant reel.

Above A diagram showing how paper is made on a papermaking machine.

Below Finished paper is wound on to huge reels.

Using paper

Every day, the world's paper mills produce thousands of reels of paper. In a week, one machine can make a sheet long enough to stretch across the Atlantic Ocean. So what happens to all this paper?

Much of it is used for printing newspapers, magazines and books. Newspapers are printed on a special paper called **newsprint**.

A lorry transporting reels of newsprint which is used to produce a national newspaper.

This is coarse and cheap to make, but soon goes yellow in the sun. Paper made for books and magazines is of better quality.

Magazines are usually made of better quality paper than newspapers.

Paper can be treated in many different ways. Wrapping paper is printed with colours and designs. Cups and cartons are covered with wax or plastic. **Photographic paper** is coated with special chemicals. Some paper is polished on a drying roller so that one side is shiny. This is called **machine-glazed paper**, and it is used for posters, carrier bags and envelopes.

Boards and boxes

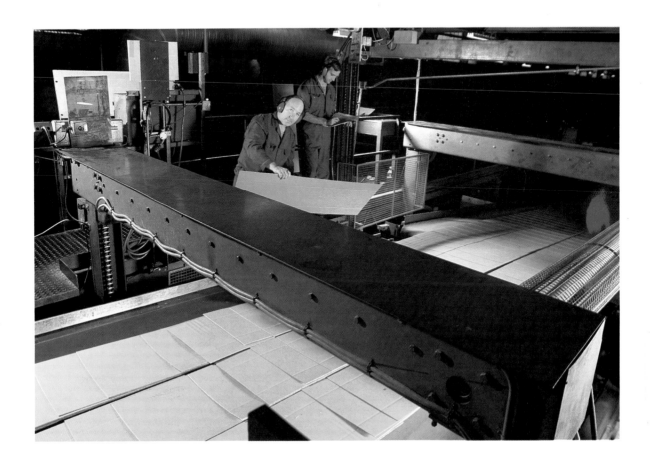

Corrugated board that has been cut and is ready for printing.

If you press several layers of pulp together, you get cardboard. This is thicker and stiffer than paper, and much stronger. Cardboard has thousands of uses. Thin, high-quality cardboard is made into index cards, postcards and greetings cards. Thicker board is used for book covers, cartons, children's games and all kinds of packaging.

Cardboard is made in a different way from paper. The pulp mixture is pumped into a tank, where there is a cylinder covered with wire mesh. The cylinder turns and picks up a mass of fibres. The water drains off, and the fibres form a sheet. As many as six or eight layers of fibres may be pressed together to make cardboard.

Corrugated board is made of three layers, just like a sandwich. The middle layer of paper is bent, or 'corrugated', and the outer layers are glued to it. Corrugated board is even stronger than cardboard.

This printed board will be made into cardboard boxes.

21

New paper from old

What do you do with old newspapers? Or wrapping paper? Or letters? You probably throw them away. But they can all be used again. The fibres in the paper can be broken down and put together to make new paper. Waste paper is now a very important part of papermaking. Some paper and boards are made by using only waste paper.

Waste paper from homes and offices is sorted, cleaned and pulped to make new paper.

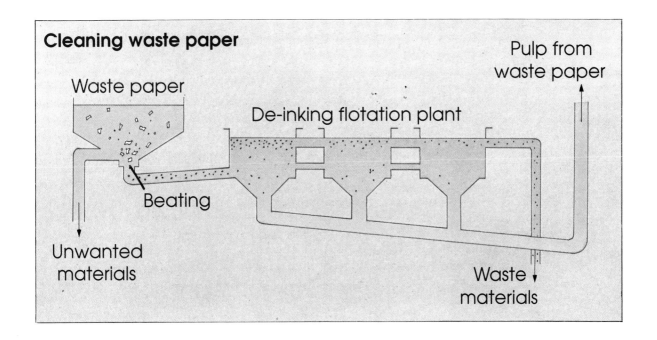

Cleaning waste paper

Waste paper

De-inking flotation plant

Pulp from waste paper

Beating

Unwanted materials

Waste materials

The main problem with waste paper is the dirt. Used paper is covered with ink and other chemicals, and can be full of staples, wire and bits of plastic. But modern machines can clean all these out.

First, the bundles of waste paper are beaten with water into a pulp. This is whirled round in a big drum, like a spin drier. The heavy pieces of metal and dirt sink to the bottom. The ink and colours are separated and the lighter fibres come out at the top. The pulp is now clean, and can be rolled and dried into paper again.

A diagram showing how dirt and inks are removed from paper ready for recycling.

The world's forests

A spruce plantation in Norway.

The paper industry needs large supplies of wood. In the past lumber companies cut down areas of natural forest for paper. In developed countries, the wood needed for paper now comes from plantations of fast-growing conifers. The paper industry claims that at least two trees are planted for every one cut down. If the planned forests are managed properly, natural forest should not need to be cut down for papermaking.

Many people, however, do not like these planted forests.

Saplings are grown from seed. They are then moved to plantations to produce wood for papermaking.

24

Tropical rainforests are cut down for timber. They also provide fuel and grazing land for cattle. The wood is not used for papermaking.

They think the forests are too thick and dark, so that few animals and plants can live there, and that conifers make the soil more acid. Other people say that the young trees are good for our planet because they help control the earth's climate.

But the world's natural forests are still in danger. In some developing countries tropical rainforest is being cut down, not for paper, but for timber to sell. The land is also cleared for farming. In dry areas trees are cut down for firewood. Without the cover of the trees, the soil is quickly washed away and the forests are replaced by deserts.

Paper and pollution

Papermaking is a complicated process which uses up a great deal of resources and energy. Beside the fibres that are needed to make paper, paper manufacturers use chemicals, clay, starch and dyes in the papermaking process.

Liquids produced from papermaking are kept in big tanks so that impurities can settle on the bottom.

A great deal of water is also used to make paper. The paper industry has to take great care to make sure that the water is cleaned before it is returned to the rivers.

Strict laws control waste from paper mills. Filters stop any harmful gases escaping into the air.

There are strict laws that control the way that industries deal with their waste liquids and gases. This prevents them harming the environment. In papermaking, special **filters** are used to prevent gases escaping into the air. Liquids that are drained from the pulp are often kept in large tanks so that **impurities** can settle on the bottom.

In many ways papermaking can be friendly to our planet. The wood it uses is renewable, and paper can be **recycled**. If paper is thrown away, it rots down in the earth. If paper is burned, it can be used as a source of energy.

These huge vessels store waste from paper mills.

Projects with paper

Make a papier mâché owl

You will need:

A balloon
Newspaper
Flour and water paste
A piece of wire gauze 15 cm sq

Brushes
Paint
A pin

1. Blow up the balloon and knot the end.

2. Mix the flour and water into paste. Tear the newspaper into short strips.

3. Brush the paste on to the paper strips and stick them on to the balloon. Put one layer in one direction, and the next layer in another direction. Cover the balloon with five or six layers of the mixture.

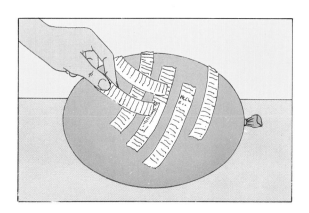

4. Leave it to dry overnight. Then paint it like an owl, with two big eyes, a beak and wings. You may need to pop the balloon to make your owl stand upright.

Recycle your own paper

You will need:

Waste paper
Blotting paper
Warm water
A piece of wire gauze 15 cm sq

A bowl
An egg beater
A rolling pin

1. Tear the paper into pieces. Put the pieces in the bowl with the warm water.

2. Leave the mixture to soak for ten minutes. Then beat it together with the egg beater.

3. Dip the gauze into the bowl. Lift it up flat and let the water drain off.

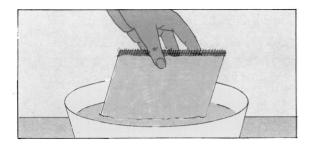

4. Gently turn the gauze upside down over a sheet of blotting paper.

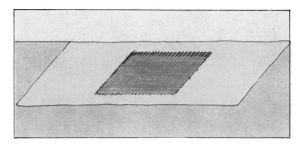

5. Remove the gauze and put a piece of blotting paper on top.

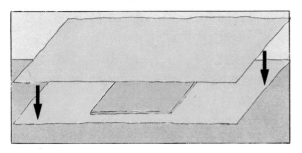

6. Roll the sheets with a rolling pin, and ask a grown-up to iron them.

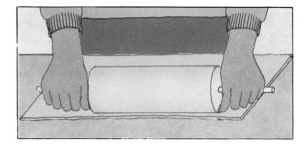

When they are dry, take off the top sheet and peel off your new, recycled paper.

Glossary

Bleach The process which removes the colour from paper and purifies it.

Calender The last heavy roller on the papermaking machine which gives paper its smooth finish.

Cellulose The material that makes up the cell walls of plants.

Chipper A huge drum in which timber is cut into chips.

Fibres The tiny, hair-like strands that make up trees and other plants.

Filter A very fine mesh, or something with tiny holes that prevents unwanted substances passing through it.

Flow head A series of nozzles which spread the pulp on to a mesh screen.

Forester A person trained to look after a forest and plant young trees.

Hardwood A type of tree with broad leaves. Most hardwoods are deciduous, which means they shed their leaves in winter.

Impurities Unwanted matter, such as dirt and grit.

Knot A lump of hard tissues that forms on the trunks of some trees.

Machine-glazed paper Paper which has been polished on one side by a special roller.

Mesh Criss-crossed wires or threads, which have tiny holes between each other.

Newsprint Coarse, cheap paper used to make newspapers.

Papyrus A water reed, weaved into paper-like material by the Ancient Egyptians.

Photographic paper Paper coated with chemicals which make it sensitive to light.

Pulp A mixture of broken-down fibres and water.

Recycled Treating materials that have been used before so that they can be used again.

Refiner A tank in which the pulp is beaten to fluff out the fibres.

Size A kind of glue which is used as a coating for paper to stop it absorbing ink.

Softwood A type of tree which bears cones and has thin, needle-like leaves. Most softwoods are evergreen.

Vacuum box A box which sucks water out of the wet pulp.

Books to read

Dixon, Annabelle **Paper** (A & C Black, 1988)
Lambert, Mark **Focus on Paper** (Wayland, 1986)
Limousin, Edile **The Story of Paper** (Moonlight, 1986)
Perrins, Lesley **Paper** (Faber, 1985)
Wood, Tim **Making Paper** (Franklin Watts, 1987)

Useful addresses

Australia
Pulp and Paper Manufacturers
    Federation of Australia
GPO Box 1469N
Melbourne
Victoria 3001

Canada
Canadian Pulp and Paper
    Association
Sun Life Building, 19th Floor
1155 Metcalfe Street
Montreal
PQ H3B 4T6

New Zealand
New Zealand Pulp and Paper
    Industry Association Inc
PO Box 1650
Trust Bank Building 7th Floor
Hinemoa Street
Rotorua

UK
Pulp and Paper Information Centre
Papermakers House
Rivenhall Road
Westlea
Swindon
SN5 7BE

Scott Ltd
Scott House
Wood Street
East Grinstead
West Sussex
RN19 1UR

USA
American Paper Institute
260 Madison Avenue
New York 10016

Index

acid soil 25
Ancient Egyptians 8
art paper 7

bark 12
bleaching 13
books 4, 19

calenders 17
cardboard 4, 20, 21, 22
cellulose 6
chemicals 12, 19, 23, 26
chipper 12
clay 15, 26
conifers 10, 24

drying cylinders 17

energy 26, 27
envelopes 19
environment 27

fibres 6, 7, 14, 15, 16, 21, 22, 23, 26
filters 27

flow head 16
forests 10, 12, 24, 25

gases 27

hardwoods 11
hemp 7
high-quality paper 7

impurities 27

loggers 11

machine-glazed paper 19
magazines 19
manila 7
mesh 16, 17, 21

newsprint 18, 19

packaging 20
papermaking machine 9, 16, 17
paper mill 13, 14, 15, 18
papier mâché 28

papyrus 8
photographic paper 19
printing 9, 19
pulp mill 12, 13

rags 7
recycling 22, 23, 27
refiner 15

size 15
softwoods 11

tropical rainforests 25
T'sai Lun 8

vacuum boxes 17

waste liquids 27
waste paper 14, 22, 23
wrapping paper 19, 22

Picture acknowledgements

The publishers would like to thank the following for allowing their photographs to be reproduced in this book: Bruce Coleman Ltd 6 bottom (Thomas Buchholz), 10 (Mark N. Boulton), 13 (Frans Lanting), 24 top (Dr Eckart Pott); E. T. Archive 8 (top); the Hutchison Library 19; J Allan Cash Ltd *cover* (top), 7, 8 (bottom), 11 (bottom), 18, 24 (bottom); Tony Stone Worldwide *cover* (bottom), 11 (top) 25, 27 (top); Wayland Picture Library pictures by Angus Blackburn, *title page*, 4, 5, 14, 15 (both), 16, 17, 20, 21, 22, 26, 27 (bottom), others 6 (top), 9. Artwork on pages 12-13, 17, 23 by Marilyn Clay, pages 28, 29 by Jenny Hughes.